A Note to Parents

DK READERS is a compelling program for beginning readers, designed in conjunction with leading literacy experts, including Dr. Linda Gambrell, Director of the School of Education at Clemson University. Dr. Gambrell has served on the Board of Directors of the International Reading Association and as President of the National Reading Conference.

Beautiful illustrations and superb full-color photographs combine with engaging, easy-to-read stories to offer a fresh approach to each subject in the series. Each DK READER is guaranteed to capture a child's interest while developing his or her reading skills, general knowledge, and love of reading.

The four levels of DK READERS are aimed at different reading abilities, enabling you to choose the books that are exactly right for your child:

Level 1: Beginning to read
Level 2: Beginning to read alor
Level 3: Reading alone
Level 4: Proficient readers

D1055941

The "normal" age at which a child begins to read can be anywhere from three to eight years old, so these levels are intended only as a general guideline.

No matter which level you select, you can be sure that you are helping your child learn to read, then read to learn!

DK

LONDON, NEW YORK, MUNICH,
MELBOURNE, AND DELHI

Project Editor Deborah Murrell
Art Editor Catherine Goldsmith
Senior Art Editor Sarah Ponder
Managing Editor Bridget Gibbs
Senior DTP Designer Bridget Roseberry
US Editor Regina Kahney
Production Melanie Dowland
Picture Researcher Frances Vargo
Picture Librarian Sally Hamilton
Jacket Designer Margherita Gianni

Reading Consultant
Linda Gambrell, Ph.D.

First American Edition, 2000
09 10 11 12 13 20 19 18 17 16 15 14 13 12
Published in the United States by DK Publishing, Inc.
375 Hudson Street, New York, New York 10014

Published in Great Britain by Dorling Kindersley Limited

Library of Congress Cataloging-in-Publication Data
Thomson, Ruth, 1949-
    Dinosaur's Day / by Ruth Thomson. -- 1st American ed.
    p.   cm. -- (Dorling Kindersley readers. Level 1)
    Summary: A gentle Triceratops forgets to stay with the herd and
has to use his sharp horns to fight a Tyrannosaurus.
    ISBN:978-0-7894-6634-1(pb)ISBN:978-0-7894-6635-8(hc)
    [1. Dinosaurs -- Fiction.]
    I. Title. II. Series.
PZ7.T38 Di 2000
[Fic] -- dc21   00-027355
                                          CIP
                                          AC

Color reproduction by Colourscan, Singapore
Printed and bound in China by L Rex Printing Co., Ltd.

The publisher would like to thank the following for their kind
permission to reproduce their images:
Photography: Dave King, John Downs 14
Illustrations: Simone Boni/L.R. Galante
Natural History Museum: 8-9, 11, 12-13, 14, 15, 21
Ardea London Ltd.: Arthur Hayward 16-17
All other images © Dorling Kindersley
For further information see www.dkimages.com

Discover more at

www.dk.com

 **DK READERS**

BEGINNING
TO READ

1

Dinosaur's Day

Written by Ruth Thomson

A Dorling Kindersley Book

I am Triceratops.

I am a dinosaur.

I am big and strong.

Triceratops
(try-SER-uh-tops)

I have three spiky horns
on my head.
I have a bony frill
on my neck.

frill

I look fierce,
but I am gentle.

beak

I spend all day eating plants.
I snip off twigs and leaves
with my hard beak.

I live in a group
called a herd.
We keep watch
for fierce dinosaurs.
They might want to eat us!

All sorts of other dinosaurs
live near the river with us.

Everything is peaceful.

All of a sudden,
what do I see?

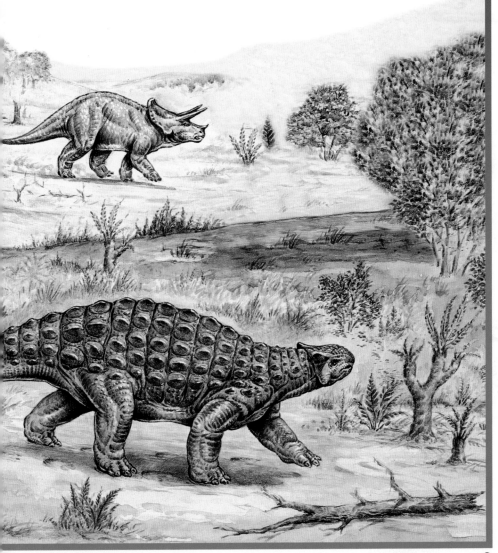

A Tyrannosaurus!
He is the fiercest dinosaur of all.

Tyrannosaurus
(tie-RAN-uh-SORE-us)

He has strong toes
and sharp claws.
He has a huge mouth
full of sharp teeth.

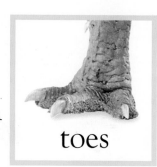

toes

A herd of light-footed dinosaurs
spots Tyrannosaurus too.
They run away on their long legs
as fast as they can.
They hide in the forest.

Ornithomimus
(OR-ni-thoh-MEE-mus)

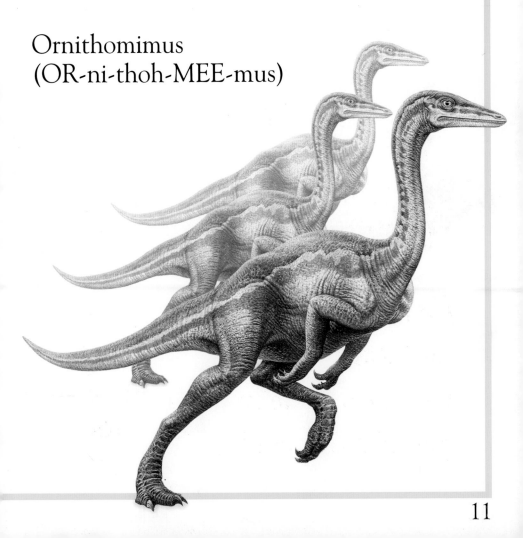

The duck-billed dinosaurs
stop eating.
They watch Tyrannosaurus.
If he comes too close,
they will run away.

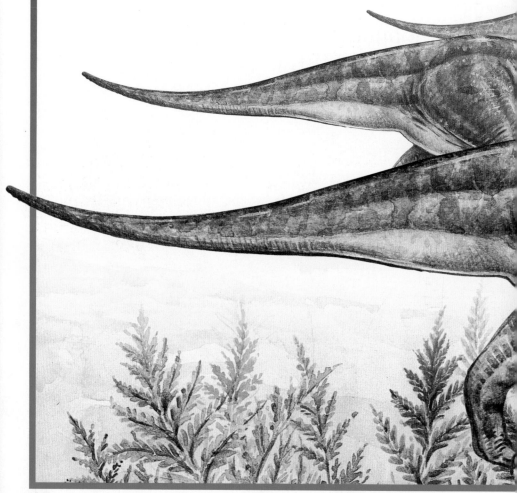

bill

Edmontosaurus
(ed-MON-tuh-SORE-us)

13

The bone-headed dinosaur
looks up and sniffs the air.
He can smell Tyrannosaurus.
If Tyrannosaurus
comes too close,
he will run away too.

Pachycephalosaurus
(PAK-ee-SEF-uh-low-SORE-us)

14

The dinosaurs with head crests
hoot in alarm.

Parasaurolophus
(par-uh-sore-OLL-uh-fuss)

crest

The armored dinosaur has a club
on the end of his tail.
He gets ready to swing it
at Tyrannosaurus.

club

Ankylosaurus
(an-KIE-luh-SORE-us)

I am busy watching
all the other dinosaurs.
I forget to stay with my herd.

I can see Tyrannosaurus.
He can see me.

Tyrannosaurus runs towards me.
He looks hungry.
His eyes are glinting.

teeth

His mouth is open.
I can see his sharp teeth.

Thud!
Thud!

He comes nearer
and nearer.

Tyrannosaurus
stands up.
He is very tall.
He lifts his head
and roars loudly.

Tyrannosaurus is trying
to scare me,
but I am not scared.
I have my sharp horns
for fighting.
I have my bony frill
to protect me.

I lower my head.
I bellow loudly.
Ready, set,
here I come!
Perhaps I can stab
Tyrannosaurus
with my sharp horns.

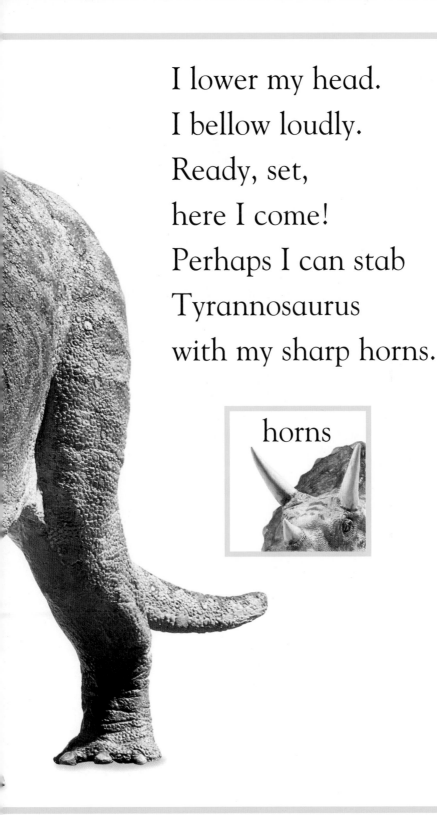

horns

Tyrannosaurus tries to bite me
with his sharp teeth.
I am still not scared.
I kick up the dust.
I try to stab him.

Tyrannosaurus is getting tired.
He stops fighting and turns away.
He goes to look for
a smaller dinosaur
for his dinner.

Now I am safe.

I am going to look for my herd.

I am very hungry
after all that fighting.

I am glad to be back
with my herd
by the river.

The other dinosaurs
come back to the river as well.
They eat peacefully.

I hope Tyrannosaurus
won't come back again.

Picture word list

frill

page 5

crest

page 15

beak

page 6

club

page 17

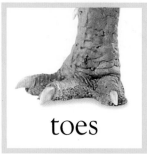
toes

page 10

teeth

page 20

bill

page 13

horns

page 25